Chief Joseph's People and Their War

By Alvin M. Josephy, Jr.

Illustration by Bill Chapman

Published by
The Yellowstone Association
for Natural Science, History & Education, Inc.
©1964

in cooperation with
NATIONAL PARK SERVICE
U.S. DEPARTMENT OF THE INTERIOR

The home of Young Joseph's band of Nez Perce Indians in the Wallowa Valley of northeastern Oregon. He had been told: "Never sell the bones of your father and mother".

Chief Joseph's People and their War*

by

ALVIN M. JOSEPHY, JR.

In June, 1877, just one year after the Custer debacle, a new and unexpected Indian outbreak flared in the West. To an American public wearied and disgusted with a governmental policy, or lack of policy, that seemed to breed Indian wars, this one, an uprising by formerly peaceful Nez Perces of Oregon and Idaho, was dramatized by what appeared to be superb Indian generalship. One army detachment after another, officered by veterans of the Civil War, floundered in battle with the hostiles. Western correspondents telegraphed the progress of a great, 1,300-mile fighting retreat by the Indians, swaying popular imagination in behalf of the valiant Nez Perces and one of their leaders, Chief Joseph, who, as handsome and noble in appearance as a Fenimore Cooper Indian, was elevated in the public opinion into something of a combined national hero and military genius.

The government received no laurels, either, as the long trail of bitter injustices that had originally driven the Nez Perces to hostility became known. The war, like more Indian troubles, had stemmed from a conflict over land. For centuries the Nez Perces had occupied the high, grassy hills and canyon-scarred plateau land where Washington, Oregon, and Idaho come together. A strong and intelligent people, they had lived in peace and friendship with the whites ever since the coming of Lewis and Clark in 1805, and it was their proud boast that no member of the tribe had ever killed a white man.

In 1855, as settlers began to appear in their country, the government called on them to cede part of their land. The Nez Perces willingly accepted the confines of a reservation, but five years later gold was discovered on the reserve, miners poured in, and in 1863 the government attempted to reduce the reservation to less than one-fourth of its previous size. Led by a chief named Lawyer, those bands whose homes already lay within the boundaries of the new reservation agreed to sign the treaty. But the other chiefs, representing about two-thirds of the tribe, protested and withdrew from the council without signing.

Among the latter was a prominent old chief named Wellamotkin, father of Chief Joseph and known to the whites as Old Joseph. His band, composed of about sixty males and perhaps twice that number of women and children, had dwelt for generations in the Wallowa

---

*The material presented here appeared as "The Last Stand of Chief Joseph", in **American Heritage,** Vol. IX, No. 2 (February, 1958), pp. 36-43 and 78-81; it is reprinted by permission of the American Heritage Publishing Company.

Valley in the northeastern corner of Oregon. Isolated on all sides by formidable natural barriers of high mountain ranges and some of the deepest gorges on the continent, the valley's lush alpine grasslands provided some of the best grazing ground in the Northwest, and settlers were particularly anxious to possess it. Old Joseph's refusal to sign the treaty of 1863, however, clouded the issue of ownership, and though the government announced that Lawyer and the chiefs who had signed had spoken for the whole tribe, binding all Nez Perces to the new reservation, no immediate attempt was made to drive Old Joseph's band from the Wallowa.

As the years went by and Old Joseph's people continued unmolested, it seemed as if their right to the Wallowa had been accepted. But white pressure against its borders increased steadily, and in 1871, as he lay dying, Old Joseph fearfully counseled his son:

"When I am gone, think of your country. You are the chief of these people. They look to you to guide them. Always remember that your father never sold his country. You must stop your ears whenever you are asked to sign a treaty selling your home. A few years more, and the white men will be all around you. They have their eyes on this land. My son, never forget my dying words. This country holds your father's body. Never sell the bones of your father and your mother."

The crisis came soon after Old Joseph's death. Settlers from Oregon's Grande Ronde found a route into the Wallowa and moved in, claiming the Indians' land. Young Joseph protested to the Indian agent on the Nez Perce reservation in Idaho, and an investigation by the Bureau of Indian Affairs resulted in a decision that the Wallowa still belonged legally to the Indians. On June 16, 1873, President Grant formally set aside the Wallowa "as a revervation for the roaming Nez Perce Indians" and ordered the whites to withdraw.

Recognition of their rights brought joy to the Indians. But it was short-lived. The settlers, refusing to move, threatened to exterminate Joseph's people if they didn't leave the valley. In defiance of the presidential order, more whites rolled in by the wagonload. As friction increased, Oregon's governor, Lafayette P. Grover, attacked Washington officials for having abandoned the government's position of 1863 and forced the Administration to reverse itself. In 1875 a new and confusing presidential edict reopened the Wallowa to white homesteaders.

The Nez Perces were dismayed. Young Joseph, whom they called Heinmot Tooyalakekt, meaning "Thunder Traveling to Loftier Mountain Heights," counseled patience. He moved the Indian camps from the neighborhood of the settlers and again appealed to the federal authorities. The assistant adjutant general of the Military Department of the Columbia, Major H. Clay Wood, was assigned to

Chief Looking Glass addressing a council of the Nez Perce chiefs. The strategy of the tribe during the retreat to the eastern buffalo lands was decided by agreement in such assemblies.

make a survey of the conflicting claims, and in his report, forwarded to Washington by his commanding officer, O. O. Howard, the one-armed "Christian" general of the Civil War, stated: "In my opinion, the non-treaty Nez Perces cannot in law be regarded as bound by the treaty of 1863, and insofar as it attempts to deprive them of a right to occupancy of any land, its provisions are null and void. The extinguishment of their title of occupancy contemplated by this treaty is imperfect and incomplete."

At first the government took no action, but as harassment of the Indians continued and the threat increased that they might retaliate with violence, a commission of five members was appointed to meet with the Nez Perces in November, 1876, with authority to make a final settlement of the matter for "the welfare of both whites and Indians."

The commissioners, Howard, Wood, and three eastern civilians, found Joseph a disquieting figure. Only 36 years old, tall and powerfully built, he seemed strangely amicable and gentle; yet he bore himself with the quiet strength and dignity of one who stood in awe of no man. And when he spoke, it was with an eloquent logic that nettled the whites, who found themselves resenting their inability to dominate him.

Why, they asked him, did he refuse to give up the Wallowa? He answered by referring to the land as the Mother of the Indians, something that could not be sold or given away. "We love the land," he said, "It is our home." But, they persisted, Lawyer had signed it away in 1863.

Joseph had a ready reply that embarrassed them. "I believe the old treaty has never been correctly reported," he said. "If we ever owned the land we own it still, for we never sold it. In the treaty councils the commissioners have claimed that our country has been sold to the government. Suppose a white man should come to me and say, 'Joseph, I like your horses, and I want to buy them.' I say to him, 'No, my horses suit me, I will not sell them.' Then he goes to my neighbor, and says to him, 'Joseph has some good horses. I want to buy them but he refuses to sell.' My neighbor answers, 'Pay me the money, and I will sell you Joseph's horses.' The white man returns to me and says, 'Joseph, I have bought your horses and you must let me have them.' If we sold our lands to the government, this is the way they were bought."

To all their arguments, Joseph replied with an uncompromising "No" and when the council ended, the exasperated commissioners had made no progress with him. But events were moving against the Indians. The situation in the Wallowa had grown perilous, and the commission was under political pressure. Two excited white men had killed an Indian youth after mistakenly accusing him of stealing their horses. Joseph had had all he could do to keep his people calm, and the settlers, fearing an uprising, were arming and calling for military protection.

To the commissioners, despite the fact that it was unjust and there was no legal basis for it, there could be only one decision, and before they left the reservation headquarters at Lapwai, they rendered it: Unless, within a reasonable time, all the non-treaty Nez Perces (the other bands that had not signed in 1863, as well as Joseph's people in the Wallowa) voluntarily came onto the reservation, **they should be placed there by force.** General Howard, symbolizing the force that would be used, signed the report along with the three easterners. Only Major Wood's name was absent, and it is believed that he submitted a minority report, though it has never been found.

Immediately after the decision, the Indian Bureau defined the "reasonable time" and ordered the Indians to come onto the reservation by April 1, 1877. Unable to move their herds and villages across the rugged canyons in the dead of winter, the Nez Perces appealed for another conference, and, as April 1 came and went, General Howard agreed to one last meeting with all the non-treaty chiefs at Lapwai. It did no good. The die had been cast, and Howard adamantly refused to discuss the commission's decision. As the Indians pleaded in proud but pitiable terms to be allowed to remain in the lands where their fathers were buried, the General finally lost patience and threw one of the most respected old chiefs, a deeply religious war leader and tribal orator named Toohoolhoolzote, into the guardhouse. It broke the spirit of the others. To gain Toohoolhoolzote's release, they capitulated with bitterness and agreed to have their bands on the reservation in thirty days.

All of Joseph's skill as a diplomat had to be called into play when he returned to his people. He had abandoned his father's counsel and trust, and there were cries to ignore him and go to war rather than move to the reservation. When Joseph argued that the white man's power was far too great for them to resist and that it was "better to live at peace than to begin a war and lie dead," they called him a coward. But he received strong assistance from his younger brother, Ollokot, a daring and courageous buffalo hunter and warrior who had won many tribal honors and held the respect of the more belligerent younger element. Eventually the two brothers won agreement to the capitulation from the band's council. With heavy hearts, the Indians prepared to round up their stock and move.

A half year's work was crowded into less than thirty days as the people combed the mountains and forests for their animals and drove them down the steep draws to the Snake. The river was in flood, and hundreds of head of stock were swept away and drowned during the tumultuous crossing. Other portions of the herds, left behind on the bluffs and plateau, were silently appropriated by white settlers as the Indians withdrew. By June 2, with twelve days of grace remaining, the people reached an ancient tribal rendevous area just outside the border of the reservation. Here they joined the other non-treaty bands and lingered for a last bit of freedom.

It was a fatal pause. On June 12 the Indians staged a parade through the camp, and one of the young men named Wahlitits, whose father had been murdered by a white man two years before, was taunted by an old warrior for having allowed the slaying to go unavenged. The next morning, his honor as a man impugned, Wahlitits stole away with two companions. By nightfall, in an outpouring of long-suppressed hatred, the youths had killed four white men along the Salmon River and wounded another one, all notorious for their hostility to the Nez Perces. The young men returned to the camp, announced what they had done and raised a bigger party that continued the raids during the next two days, killing fourteen or fifteen additional whites and striking terror among the settlers and miners of central Idaho.

Both Joseph and Ollokot had been absent from the camp during the first raid, butchering cattle on the opposite side of the Salmon River. They returned home in horror, finding the camp in confusion and the older people crying with fear and striking their tepees, intending to scatter to hiding places. Most of the Indians were certain that there would now be war, but Joseph still hoped to avert it. He tried to calm his people, assuring them that General Howard would not blame the whole tribe for the irresponsible actions of a few of it's young hot-heads, and urged them to remain where they were and await the troops, with whom he would make a settlement. The situation, however, had gone too far. The warriors rode around the camp, crying out that they would now give General Howard the fight that he had wanted, and the people would not listen to Joseph. One by one the bands departed to a hiding place farther south, in White Bird Canyon, leaving behind only Joseph, Ollokot, and a few of the Wallowa Indians.

Joseph's wife had given birth to a daughter while he had been across the Salmon, and he lingered with her now in their tepee. Several warriors were detailed to watch him and Ollokot, lest these leaders who had so often pleaded for peace would desert the nontreaties and move onto the reservation. But though he had vigorously opposed war, Joseph would not abandon his people; two days later he and Ollokot, resolved to fight now that hostilities seemed unavoidable, joined the non-treaties in the new camp at White Bird.

Back at Lapwai Howard was stunned by news of the Salmon River outbreaks. He had planned all winter against trouble in the Wallowa, and when Joseph had moved out peacefully, he had thought that all danger was past. At the news of the outbreaks, he hastily ordered two troops of the 1st Cavalry, that had been stationed at Lapwai, ninety troopers and four officers under Captain David Perry and Captain Joel Trimble, to round up the hostiles and force them onto the reservation. Eleven civilian volunteers and twelve treaty Nez Perces accompanied the troops, and after a rapid two days' march of almost eighty miles, they learned of the Nez Perce camp in White Bird Canyon and prepared to attack it early the following morning.

Alert Indian spies warned the Nez Perces of the troops' approach. The soldiers would have to descend a long draw of treeless, rolling land, flanked by ridges and hills, to reach the Nez Perce village, which lay behind two buttes at the bottom of the slope. The chiefs were uncertain whether to resist and detailed six men to take a flag of truce forward and try to arrange a peaceful meeting with the officers. At the same time, the old men, women, and children were ordered to drive in the camp's stock, while the warriors, stripping for action and mounting their ponies, sought hiding places to the right and left of the draw to await events. The total manpower of the Indian bands was about 150, but many of the men that morning were lying in camp, drunk on whisky seized during the raids and unable to fight. Others had no weapons or were too old, sick, or frightened to use them. Altogether, not more than 60 or 70 Indians-armed with bows and arrows; shotguns; old, muzzleloading, fur-trade muskets; and a few modern rifles-rode out to defend the village.

The nature of the terrain, offering a multitude of hiding places for flanking attacks, should have put the troopers on their guard. Instead they trotted confidently down the draw, ready for a thundering surprise charge. As they rounded a small hill, the Indian truce team appeared directly ahead of them. Behind the men with the white flag were other Nez Perces, sitting on their horses waiting to see what would happen. There was an instant of surprise. Then a volunteer raised his rifle and shot at the truce team. The Indians backed away, unharmed, a Nez Perce behind them fired in return, killing one of Perry's two trumpeters, and the fight was on. As Indians began shooting from all directions, Perry hastily deployed his men in a line across the draw, placing the volunteers on a high, rocky knoll to his left. The company in the center dismounted, letting men in the rear hold their horses, and the company on the right remained mounted.

The battle, fought without plan by the Indians, lasted only a few moments. On the left, a small body of Nez Perces swept from behind a hill and galloped straight at the volunteers, sending them flying in panic back up the draw and exposing Perry's whole line. At the same time Ollokot, leading a large number of warriors, emerged from cover on the right and, firing as he came, charged into Perry's mounted troop, frightening the horses and disorganizing the soldiers. The men in the center, seeing Indians and confusion all around them, gave way and made a sudden rush for their horses. In a few minutes the entire command was cut into small groups fighting desperately for their lives. Nineteen men under Lieutenant Edward Theller tried to make a stand but were driven against a rocky wall and wiped out. The rest of the troop disintegrated into a fleeing rabble and got away, leaving behind them a total of 34 dead, a third of Perry's command. The Indians had only two men wounded and none killed; equally important for the future, they retrieved from the battlefield 63 rifles and a large number of pistols.

Perry's defeat spread alarm throughout the settlements of the Northwest and angered the rest of the nation, to whom the Custer massacre was still fresh. Howard was shocked and, fearing that the uprising would spread to the treaty Nez Perces as well as other Northwest tribes, called for troop reinforcements from all over the West. Men were started inland from Portland and San Francisco, artillerymen returning from Alaska were diverted up the Columbia, and from as far away as Atlanta, Georgia, infantry units were entrained for the scene of the new Indian outbreak.

Within a week Howard himself took the field. With a force of 227 hastily assembled troops, 20 civilians, and a large group of packers and guides, he marched hurriedly out from Lapwai, intending to punish the hostiles. The Indians, reinforced by a small band that had just returned from the Montana buffalo plains under the leadership of two redoubtable warriors, Five Wounds and Rainbow, had withdrawn from White Bird and, when Howard caught up with them, had crossed with all their equipment and pony herds to the relative safety of the south bank of the Salmon. For a while the two groups faced each other from opposite sides of the wilderness river while Howard planned how to get his troops across the turbulent stream and catch the Indians before they could retreat into the rocky wilds of central Idaho. From his rear he received false information from excited settlers that a large band of hitherto peaceful Nez Perces, under a famous tribal war chief named Looking Glass, was planning to leave the reservation and join the hostiles. Accepting the information as true, he divided his forces and sent Captain Stephen Whipple with two troops of cavalry to intercept Looking Glass.

It was a disastrous move. As Whipple departed, Howard received boats and started across the river, only to see the Indians move off into the wilderness ahead of him. For several days he was led on a wearying, frustrating chase through mud and driving rain, up and down steep hills and mountain slopes, and across some of the most rugged terrain in the West. Meanwhile Whipple reached Looking Glass's village on the reservation and, although he found it peaceful, launched a vicious assault upon it. The startled Indians, struck without warning, fled across a river to the shelter of some trees, where they were rallied by their outraged chief. Rumors now came to Whipple that the main band of Indians had somehow evaded General Howard, had recrossed the Salmon, and were between him and the General, threatening his own rear, Howard's supply lines, and all the settlements on the Camas Prairie which he was supposed to be protecting.

The rumors this time were true. With Howard's troops floundering in the wilds, the non-treaties had managed to cross again to the northside of the Salmon. Howard tried to follow them, couldn't get his men and equipment across the river, and had to go back over the entire dreadful mountain trail to the place of his original crossing, where he had left his boats. Meanwhile Whipple, forgetting Looking Glass in the face of the full Nez Perce force, sent out a reconnoitering party of ten men under Lieutenant S. M. Rains and dug in for an expected attack. The Indians wiped out Rains' party to a man, cut up another group of scouts and several hastily formed bodies of civilian volunteers, and finally, bypassing Whipple and the terrified settlers barricaded in Cottonwood and Grangeville, moved to another hiding place on the South Fork of the Clearwater River. Here they were joined by Looking Glass's infuriated band. It gave the Indians another forty fighting men but also raised the number of women and children, who would have to be carried along and protected from the soldiers, to a peak figure of 450.

From the beginning it had been assumed by the whites that Joseph, spokesman for the non-treaties in peacetime, had also been leading them in war. Howard had credited him with skillfully contriving the ambush of Perry at White Bird. Now Joseph was being given grudging praise for the masterful way in which the Indians had evaded Howard in the wilderness and doubled back to get between him and Whipple. In addition, the Nez Perces had been conducting themselves in an unusual manner for Indians "on the warpath," refraining from scalping or mutilating bodies, treating white women and noncombatants with humanity and even friendliness, and otherwise adhering to what was considered the white man's code of war. This too was credited to Joseph, whose dignity and decency at prewar councils were recalled by Howard and the Indian agents.

The truth was that Nez Perce successes were resulting from a combination of overconfidence and mistakes on the part of the whites, the rugged terrain that made pursuit difficult, and, to a very great extent, the Indians' intense courage and patriotic determination to fight for their rights and protect their people. Indian strategy and tactics had also played a role, but at each step of the way these were agreed upon in councils of all the chiefs and were carried out on the field by the younger war leaders and their warriors. Joseph sat in the councils, but since he had never been a war chief his advice carried less weight than that of men like Five Wounds, Toohoolhoolzote, and Rainbow. On the march and in battle Joseph took charge of the old men, women, and children, an assignment of vital importance and sacred trust, while Ollokot and the experienced war chiefs led the young men on guard duty or in combat. The whites had no way of knowing this, and, as events continued to unfold, the legend that Nez Perce strategy was planned and executed by one man, Joseph, was spread far and wide by the hapless Army officers opposing him and accepted without question by correspondents and the U. S. public.

On July 11, with a reinforced army of 400 soldiers and 180 scouts, packers, and teamsters, Howard was back in pursuit of the Nez Perces. Suddenly he sighted their camp lying below him on the opposite side of the Clearwater River, opened fire with a four inch howitzer and two Gatling guns, and prepared to launch an attack. The Nez Perces were taken by surprise, but old Toohoolhoolzote and 24 warriors raced across the river, scaled a bluff to the level of the soldiers, and, taking shelter behind boulders, engaged the troopers with a fierce and accurate fire that held them up until more Indians could come across and get into the fight. The firing was sharp on both sides, but as increasing numbers of mounted Nez Perces began appearing over the top of the bluff to circle the troops' rear and flanks, Howard hastened his men into a square and ordered them to dig in on the open, rocky ground with their trowel bayonets.

The fighting raged all day and continued in the same spot the next morning, an almost unprecedented length of time for Indians to maintain battle in one location. The Nez Perces, outnumbered almost six to one and occasionally under artillery fire, kept the troopers pinned down and on the defensive with marksmanship that Howard's adjutant, Major C. E. S. Wood, described as "terribly accurate and very fatal." Several times small groups of Indians darted forward to engage the soldiers in hand-to-hand fights, and once they almost captured Howard's supply train. In addition, the Nez Perces held the only

The Nez Perce retreat covered 1,300 miles in about four

aths. Miles cut them off just short of Canada and safety.

spring in the area and controlled access to the river; under the blazing July sun the soldiers suffered unmercifully from thirst.

By noon of the second day the chiefs had decided that there had been enough fighting without decision. Many of the warriors had become restless and tired and wanted to leave. Holding the line long enough for Joseph to get the families packed and safely away with the herds, the Indians, one by one, ceased fighting and withdrew down the bluff. Howard's troops followed the last of them across the river and through the abandoned camp. It was an anti-climactic and hollow finish to a battle that had cost the army thirteen killed and twenty-seven wounded, two of them fatally. Howard could count four Indians killed and six wounded, but the hostiles had escaped from him again.

The Nez Perces crossed the Clearwater north of the troops and paused at an old meeting ground on the Weippe Prairie to decide what to do next. They had had enough of Howard and thought that if they left Idaho and went somewhere else, the General would be satisfied and would leave them alone. Looking Glass, who many times had hunted buffalo and fought with the Crows in Montana, urged that they cross the mountains and join that tribe. They could then hunt on the plains in peace, he told them, and the war would be over. It was a harsh proposal, for it meant the final abandonment of their homeland, but with the people's safety weighing heavily on them Joseph and the other chiefs reluctantly agreed to the exodus. On July 16, having named Looking Glass as supreme chief for the trek to the Crows, the bands set off on the arduous Lolo Trail across the wild and precipitous heights of the Bitterroot Mountains.

Smarting under increasing criticism from Washington, as well as from the press and public, Howard once more took after the Indians, doggedly following their trail up through the thick and tangled forest growth of mountain slopes to the high, ridge-top route that led from Idaho to Montana. It was a painful and grueling trip for both pursuers and pursued. The Indian families, stumbling along over steep and rocky trails, guarded by the warriors and driving some 2,000 horses with them, managed to keep well ahead of the troops, who, with their guns and camp equipment, found the going even rougher. In the meantime word of the Indian flight had been telegraphed ahead to Montana, and from Missoula Captain Charles C. Rawn, with 35 men of the 7th Infantry and 200 citizen volunteers from the Bitterroot Valley, hastened to the eastern end of the Lolo Trail and threw up a log fort from which to block the hostiles' passage until Howard could catch up to them from the rear.

On July 25, after nine days in the mountains, the Nez Perces appeared above Rawn's fort, and Joseph, Looking Glass, and an elderly chief named White Bird came down for a parley. Explaining that they were on their way to the Crows, the Indians promised to move peacefully through the Bitterroot Valley, respecting the settlements and paying for any supplies they needed. It satisfied the volunteers, who having no stomach for an Indian fight, deserted Rawn and stole back to their homes. As a federal officer, Rawn was obliged to continue his posture of resistance, but fortunately for his depleted garrison the Indians shrewdly bypassed his fort and, making a noisy feint in front of him, quietly filed around him on another mountain trail that led them into the Bitterroot Valley. The embarrassed Captain withdrew to Missoula, and his log bastion was promptly dubbed Fort Fizzle by the many wags who were beginning to root for Joseph and the apparently unconquerable Nez Perces.

Moving through the heavily settled valley, the Indians scrupulously maintained their promise to commit no hostile act. At Stevensville they paused to buy coffee, flour, sugar, and tobacco and paid the merchants with gold dust and currency. The friendly treatment they received from the Montana citizens made the Indians believe that, now they were out of Idaho, the war was over and they were safe. They moved leisurely south to the Big Hole Valley and, on an open meadow beside the willow-lined Big Hole River, pitched camp to rest.

The Big Hole Battlefield as it appears now from the Indian snipers' position at the Twin Trees. The Nez Perce village, which stood in the meadow beyond the line of brush, was attacked by troops who charged across the river from the base of this hill.

Howard was still far back in the Bitterroots, temporarily out of the picture. But, unknown to the Nez Perces, a new force of 163 army regulars and 35 volunteers under Colonel John Gibbon was hurrying across country from Fort Shaw, on the Sun River, by forced marches to attack them. On the night of August 8 Gibbon gained a wooded hill above the unsuspecting Nez Perce camp and, the next morning at dawn, launched a surprise attack. Firing volleys into the sleeping village, the soldiers charged down the hill in a long line, forded the shallow river, and swept into the camp, shooting and clubbing men, women, and children. Some of the Nez Perces were able to seize their weapons and ammunition belts and escape to the shelter of the willows. There they were rallied by the aged White Bird, who cried at them, "Why are we retreating? Since the world was made, brave men have fought for their women and children! Fight! Shoot them down! We can shoot as well as any of these soldiers!"

Gibbon's commanding officer on the left had been killed during the opening charge and, without a leader, that part of the line faltered as Indians stood their ground and fought back desperately from the tepees. The troopers were forced toward the right, allowing the Nez Perces in that sector to erect a firing line against them. This brought confusion to the main part of the camp, where Gibbon's men, in complete control, were unsuccessfully trying to set the leather tepees afire. With his milling troops being pushed together and soldiers being struck both by the Indians on the left and by White Bird's snipers on the right, Gibbon, who had been wounded in the leg, ordered a withdrawal across the river to the protection of the wooded knoll from which the attack had been launched. To his chagrin the Nez Perces swarmed after him, and in a few moments he found himself on the defensive, fighting fiercely, his position encircled by well-concealed Indian sharpshooters.

As the soldiers pulled out of the village, the old men, women, and children, directed by Joseph, hurried back in, picked up their dead and wounded, struck the tepees, and, driving their pack strings and pony herds ahead of them, moved off toward the south. The warriors remained behind, continuing the siege on the hill throughout the day and into the night, pinning down Gibbon's men in shallow holes and behind fallen trees, and picking off anyone who showed himself. Cut off and without prospect of relief, the soldiers' position rapidly became desperate. The men ran out of water, and cries from the unattended wounded filled the air. Gibbon's howitzer, ordered to come up after the initial attack, arrived on the scene and was immediately captured by a group of wild-charging Nez Perces, who rolled it over a steep bluff. Another body of Indians seized a packload of 2,000 rounds of Gibbon's ammunition. By eleven that night, with their camp safely away, the warriors mercifully decided to break off the engagement and spare the surviving troopers. Backing off slowly to guard against pursuit, they took the trail after Joseph.

Norma Blackeagle, a grandniece of the Chiefs Young Joseph and Looking Glass, at the place where the Radersburg tourists were captured by Nez Perce Indians in the Lower Geyser Basin of Yellowstone National Park.

Gibbon's men, cut up and dazed, were in no condition to follow. Thirty-three soldiers were dead and thirty-eight wounded. Fourteen of the seventeen officers were casualties. Howard's men, coming up hurriedly the next day, found the troops still in a state of shock, burying the dead and trying to care for the groaning wounded.

The Indians' losses at the Big Hole had also been high. Between sixty and ninety Nez Perces had lost their lives, including Rainbow, Five Wounds, and some of the tribe's most able warriors. Many of the casualties had been women and children, slain during the initial attack on the tepees. Joseph's wife had been among the seriously wounded, and Joseph had been seen fighting his way through the early part of the battle sheltering his new baby in his arms.

The Nez Perces now quickened their retreat across southwestern Montana. Gone were illusions that the whites would let them be. In their desperation to escape, only one haven seemed left to them. Like Sitting Bull, they would go to Canada and seek refuge among the tribes in the country of Queen Victoria. Canada was hundreds of miles away, but they would get there somehow. Looking Glass, blamed for the false sense of security that had led to so many deaths at the Big Hole, was relieved of command, and a tough fighter named Lean Elk, whom the whites had known as Poker Joe, was elevated to supreme chief. The column headed eastward toward Targhee Pass, which would lead the refugees over the Continental Divide to the Yellowstone, where they could turn north to Canada. West of the pass, rear-guard scouts brought word that Howard was catching up and pressing close behind them again. In a bold night attack, 28 warriors led by Ollokot and three other chiefs stole back to Howard's camp and ran off the General's entire pack string. Howard came to a dead halt, forced to scour the settlements for more animals, and the Indians hurried on, unhampered, across the Divide and into the area which five years before had become Yellowstone National Park.

A sight-seeing party, of which General William Tecumseh Sherman was a member, had just left the area, but the Nez Perces swooped up two other groups of campers and took them along. The chiefs insisted on humane treatment for the frightened tourists, who included a number of women. In time, as the Indians continued across the Park, past geysers and bubbling mudpots, the sight-seers were allowed to escape. On the eastern side of the Park, the Indians found themselves harassed by new bodies of troops, coming at them from posts on the Montana plains. One force of the 7th Cavalry under Colonel Samuel Sturgis tried to set a trap for the Indians in the upper Yellowstone Valley, but the Nez Perces fought their way skillfully through a mountain wilderness where the whites thought passage would be impossible and emerged on the Clark's Fork river in Sturgis' rear. Realizing he had been tricked, Sturgis gave chase with 300 men, following the Indians down the River to a crossing of the Yellowstone west of present-day Billings, Montana.

The Indians had passed over the River the previous afternoon, stopping long enough to capture a stagecoach from which the occupants escaped into the willows behind a stage station. The warriors had great fun, driving the incongruous-looking coach about the prairie for several hours. At Canyon Creek the bands turned north, and here, on

September 13, Sturgis' hard-riding cavalry overtook them. There was a furious fight. A rear guard of Indians, hiding behind rocks and in gullies, held off the troopers while the Nez Perce women and children drove the pack strings and herds to the protection of a narrow canyon that cut north through rimrock country. Sturgis ordered his men to dismount, an error that allowed the Indians to escape into the canyon. Later the cavalry tried to follow the Nez Perces in a running fight up the canyon, but the Indians succeeded in making pursuit difficult by blocking the canyon floor behind them with boulders and brush. At darkness, weary and running out of ammunition and rations, Sturgis gave up the chase. Three of his men had been killed and eleven wounded. The Indians counted three wounded, but the long pursuit was beginning to tell heavily on them. They too were becoming tired and dispirited, and they were losing horses. Many of the animals were going lame from the difficult trek and had to be abandoned. Others were being lost in the hurry to keep moving.

Beyond Canyon Creek their old allies, the Crows, now in service as scouts for the Army, began to attack them. The Nez Perces fought them off in running engagements and continued across the Musselshell to the Missouri River, helping themselves to army stores at a military depot on Cow Island while a frightened sergeant and twelve men looked on helplessly from behind an earthwork. Just across the Missouri, the Indians fought off a half-hearted attack by a small force from Fort Benton and hastened on across badlands and open, rolling plains to the Bear Paw Mountains. About thirty miles short of the Canadian line, exhausted by the long flight, they paused to rest, confident that they had outdistanced all pursuers.

Once more they were wrong, outflanked again by the telegraph, and this time the pause would end in their last stand. From Fort Keogh in the east, Colonel Nelson A. Miles, with nearly 600 men that included the 2nd and 7th Cavalry, the mounted 5th Infantry, and a body of Cheyenne warriors, was hastening obliquely across Montana, hoping to intercept the hostiles before they crossed the border. On the cold, blustery morning of September 30, Miles' Cheyenne scouts sighted the Nez Perce tepees in a deep hollow on the plains close to Snake Creek on the northern edge of the Bear Paw Mountains. Miles ordered an immediate attack, and the Cheyennes and 7th Cavalry, supported by the 5th Infantry, charged across the open ground toward the village.

The assault caught the Nez Perces in three groups. Some, including women and children, were on the distant side of the camp and were able to mount and flee to the north, where they scattered on the broken plains, to die from hunger and exposure or eventually to reach Canada in small, pitiful groups. Others, including Joseph, were trapped with the horses at some distance from the camp. A third group, at the village, found protection behind a low-lying ridge. These warriors, hidden behind rocks, opened a deadly fire on the attackers,

The rifle surrendered by Chief Joseph after the final battle near the Bear Paw Mountains in north-central Montana. It is now on display, with his ceremonial robe, at the Museum of the Upper Missouri in Fort Benton, Montana.

inflicting heavy casualties and sending the troopers reeling back short of the camp. Two officers and twenty-two soldiers were killed in the assault and four officers and thirty-eight enlisted men wounded.

The 2nd Cavalry, meanwhile, had been sent around the camp to capture the Nez Perce pony herd and try to cut off escape. This unit had better luck. The troopers crashed into the herd, stampeding the horses and splitting the Indians into small groups that fought back hand-to-hand or sought cover in gullies or behind rocks. A few of the Indians got away on ponies and disappeared to the north. Others, among them Joseph, crawled or fought their way back to the main body of Nez Perces, reaching the camp under cover of darkness. The troopers drove off at least a third of the horses, however, and most of the Nez Perces' remaining war leaders, including the brave Ollokot and Toohoolhoolzote, were killed in the fighting.

The heavy casualties Miles had sustained deterred him from ordering another charge, and he decided to lay siege to the village. He made one attempt to cut off the Indians from their water supply by establishing a line between the camp and the river, but the troops detailed to the task were driven back by fierce Indian resistance. As the siege settled down, both sides dug in, continuing a desultory sharpshooting fire between the lines. The weather turned bitterly cold, and the next morning five inches of snow covered the unretrieved bodies of the dead. The Indians, wounded, hungry, and cold, suffered intensely. Using hooks, knives, and pans, the people tried to dig crude shelters in the sides of the hollows. One dugout was caved in by a hit from Miles' howitzer that had been tilted back for use as a mortar, and a woman and child were buried alive.

As the siege continued, Miles grew concerned. There were rumors that Sitting Bull, with a band of Sioux, was coming to the Nez Perces' rescue from Canada. And, even if they didn't show up, Howard was getting closer, and Miles wanted the glory of Joseph's end for himself. Hoping to hurry the surrender, he hoisted a white flag over his trenches and, after negotiations with a Nez Perce who could speak English, lured Joseph across the lines. The two men parleyed amicably for a few moments, but when Joseph began to detail terms for an honorable surrender, Miles had him seized and made prisoner. The same day however, the Nez Perces captured one of Miles's officers. The next morning an exchange was agreed to, and Joseph was returned to his camp.

The siege went on amid cold and snow flurries, and on October 4 Howard reached the battlefield with a small advance party that included two treaty Nez Perces. The appearance of their old enemy, heralding the arrival of reinforcements for Miles, took the final heart out of the suffering Nez Perces. The next morning the two treaty Nez Perces crossed the line and told the chiefs that if they surrendered, they would be honorably treated and sent back to Lapwai. The chiefs held a final council. White Bird and Looking Glass still opposed surrender. Joseph pointed to the starving women and children in the shelter pits and to the babies that were crying around them. "For myself I do not care," he said. "It is for them I am going to surrender."

As the council broke up, Looking Glass was suddenly struck in the forehead by a stray bullet and killed. As the surviving warriors gathered around the slain chief, Joseph mounted a horse and, followed by several men on foot, rode slowly up the hill from the camp and across to the army lines where Howard and Miles awaited him. As he reached the officers, he dismounted and handed Miles his rifle. Then, stepping back, he adjusted his blanket to leave his right arm free and, addressing Miles, began one of the most touching and beautiful speeches of surrender ever made:

"Tell General Howard I know his heart. What he told me before I have in my heart. I am tired of fighting. Our chiefs are killed. Looking Glass is dead. Toohoolhoolzote is dead. The old men are all dead. It is the young men who say yes or no. He who led the young men is dead. It is cold and we have no blankets. The little children are freezing to death. My people, some of them, have run away to the hills, and have no blankets, no food;

no one knows where they are-perhaps freezing to death. I want to have time to look for my children and see how many I can find. Maybe I shall find them among the dead. Hear me, my chiefs. I am tired; my heart is sick and sad. From where the sun now stands, I will fight no more forever."

The fact that neither Joseph nor any other individual chief had been responsible for the outstanding strategy and masterful successes of the campaign is irrelevant. The surrender speech, taken down by Howard's adjutant and published soon afterwards, confirmed Joseph in the public's mind as the symbol of the Nez Perces' heroic, fighting retreat. Although the government failed to honor Miles' promise to send the Indians back to Lapwai, sympathy was aroused throughout the nation for Joseph's people. At first the Indians were shipped by flatboats and boxcars to unfamiliar, hot country in the Indian Territory, where many of them sickened and died. But friendly whites and sympathetic societies in the East continued to work for them, and public sentiment finally forced approval of their return to the Northwest. In 1885 Joseph and most of his band were sent to the Colville Reservation in Washington. Joseph made many attempts to be allowed to resettle in the Wallowa but each time was rebuffed. In 1904 he died, broken-hearted, an exile from the beautiful valley he still considered home.

Chief Joseph, worn by war and captivity, at his last home on the Colville Reservation in Washington. He died an exile from his beautiful Wallowa Valley.

ABOUT THE AUTHOR

Alvin M. Josephy, Jr., has been an editor for *Time* magazine and a member of the Advisory Board of *American Heritage* magazine.

He is the author of *The Patriot Chiefs* (Viking Press, 1961), *Now That the Buffalo's Gone* (Knopf, 1982) and *Red Power* (University of Nebraska Press, 1985).

YELLOWSTONE ASSOCIATION

This booklet was published by The Yellowstone Association for Natural Science, History & Education, Inc. in cooperation with the National Park Service, U.S. Department of the Interior.

The Yellowstone Association is a non-profit organization that funds and provides educational products and services for Yellowstone National Park. The Association operates educational bookstores, a field school, and a membership program. For more information, please visit our website at www.YellowstoneAssociation.org or contact us at Box 117, Yellowstone National Park, WY 82190. (877) 967-0090

Cover: Chief Joseph, Nez Perce, ca. 1904

Back Cover: Chief Joseph
Photo by Charles M. Bell, Washington, D.C.

Photographs courtesy of the Montana Historical Society, Helena, Montana